What Grows Here?

Santina Bruni

What grows here?

Cactuses grow here.

What grows here?

6

Water lilies grow here.

8

Trees grow here.

What grows here?

Wildflowers grow here.

What grows here?

Grasses grow here.

What grows here?

Seaweed grows here.